"It was definitely a pleasure for me to read this book. I'm struck by what great good the average Christian can take out of it. I believe it will be a comfort and consolation to many people in all different situations in their Christian lives."

*Pastor Louis Meyer,*
Appleton, WI

"Bill Favorite presents a unique first person commentary on the book of Jonah. The book cleverly sews many doctrines, especially justification, into a very comforting blanket that God wants to cover us with."

*Pastor Robbin Robbert,*
St. Peter Evangelical Lutheran Church,
Weyauwega, WI

# I Ran, But I Couldn't Hide

Solace, Serenity, and Joy from the Book of Jonah

## Bill Favorite

CROSSBOOKS
PUBLISHING

CrossBooks™
A Division of LifeWay
1663 Liberty Drive
Bloomington, IN 47403
www.crossbooks.com
Phone: 1-866-879-0502

First published by CrossBooks 07/19/2011

ISBN: 978-1-4627-0534-4 (sc)

Library of Congress Control Number: 2011933676

Printed in the United States of America

This book is printed on acid-free paper.

*In loving memory of David Mark Favorite,*
*a citizen of heaven, and an amazing one at that*

# Contents

# Acknowledgments

I extend my sincere gratitude and appreciation to Kenn Kremer, Louie Meyer, Gail Potratz, Robb Robbert, and K.C. Schuler for all their suggestions and recommendations. I also thank my brother Robert Favorite and my nephew Jonathan Favorite for their input and advice, and my son Kyle Favorite for his contribution.

A sincere thank you also to the excellent staff at CrossBooks for their dedicated and professional assistance in bringing this project to fruition. May God bless their continuing service in his Name.

# Introduction:
# In His Sights

The year was 2003. The man was a deposed dictator. And the hunt was on.

The Bush administration was in dogged pursuit of the former president of Iraq. Baghdad had been bombed, and Saddam Hussein had been forced to run. But it was only a matter of time before he ran out of places to hide. Captured by US forces literally underground, the despised despot was eventually tried and convicted by the Iraqi interim government for crimes against humanity and summarily executed in 2006.

Turn back the clock seventy years. On a stage closer to home, a much younger and far more nimble man was on the run.

The celebrated fugitive was a ballyhooed bank robber. Together with his gang, the infamous John Dillinger stung two dozen banks and four police stations before the noose was tightened by the FBI. The law moved in as he walked out of a theatre. He met his end when he tried to flee.

Fast forward now to recent events. Long thought to be holed up in a cave, Osama bin Laden was actually living in relative opulence in a carefully crafted compound. Ever blind to the meaning of life, liberty, and love, he lifted his eyes in time to notice the talons of a swooping American eagle. He took two bullets, and was buried at sea.

It all brings to mind a familiar expression: "You can run, but you cannot hide." Often, if not ordinarily, the saying connotes the fact that justice will eventually seek out the transgressor, like a slower version of a smart missile. As those agents of fear and terror perceived, if belatedly and recklessly so, the long arm of the law would not be waylaid just because it always seemed to have a gap to close. The hare would slip up someday, and the tortoise would have its man.

You can run, but you cannot hide—because the law of the land, while it may be scary for some, is of course necessary and beneficial for the sake of justice, peace, and good order. But I'm going to suggest that there can also be a gentler, less ominous side to that truism about the futility of living one's life with one eye on the rear-view mirror. You see, I really believe that old saying can be understood in a spiritual context as well. The reason I say that is because God has his sights on you and me, too.

Said in a moralizing kind of way, that could make God sound a whole lot like the dear old man in the red suit: "He knows when you are sleeping, he knows when you're awake; he knows if you've been bad or good, so be good for goodness' sake!" If my perception of God was something on that order, I think I might often dismiss him rather quickly from my mind.

But the truth is, I find it powerfully comforting to know that I am perpetually on the radar screen of the Most High. At times in my life, it has seemed as though I was lost at sea, drifting along pretty aimlessly on my personal journey, sometimes even clinging to a raft of my own making. But even then I was never really far from the unseen shore, and in reality I was very far from being alone.

You see, even though my life is filled with times when I've run from God in varying kinds of conscious and subconscious modes of escape, there's never been a time when I could successfully hide. No, there has never been a time when he hasn't sought me out. And that is a very good thing—because the God of Abraham, Isaac, Jacob, Esther, Mary, Lydia, you, me, and all his other children is not only a God of perfect justice, he is also, and above all, a God of perfect love. He is a gracious Lord whose undeserved love is as bottomless as his essence is unending and whose faithfulness to his promises is so sure that he continually speaks those wondrous pledges in his Word as though they are totally done deals.

The reason outlaws, war criminals, and terrorists run from justice is because they embrace something other than justice, something inherently flawed and distorted. So if in the present or the future I, too, find myself searching for something, perhaps that suggests a question. Might it be that I am fleeing something? Might it be that I am avoiding my loving God? Might it be that I have a tendency to try to dodge his plans for me and even to flee from the claim he makes on my life?

If I could stand back and follow the path of my life's journey, if I could trace the thoughts of my mind and the yearning of my heart over a lifetime, I think it could be pretty revealing. If a stranger were able to look at a map of my travels, I wonder if he could pick out the general direction. Could he make sense of my meandering path? Would he wonder what caused all the detours? Would he ask me, "Why all the distractions? What latent fears, what gnawing uncertainties were you harboring?"

Would he recognize my "drugs of choice" and wonder what in the world was the appeal? Would he wonder why I would ever want to wander in such directions when in reality there was a mountain of blessing for the taking right smack in front of my eyes, if only I would not take them off the safe, sensible, and secure path of God's loving will?

Running from God leads to lots of questions. What my eyes and ears so often focus on, what my senses so often seek, what my mind and heart long for—is that something I have attained or now possess? Have I found what I was looking for? Do I have it? Do I have anything, any fruits of my search? If so, is it something that will last? And what kind of value does it have?

Or, on the other hand, do I perhaps feel as though I have nothing? Have I perhaps not only gained nothing, but experienced loss as well? Have I perhaps even lost a great deal?

Perhaps this strikes a chord with you, too; or maybe, on the other hand, you have been hurt. Are you lonely or afraid? Do you feel rejected, spurned, unloved?

If any of this is true, be assured that you are not alone. Many have traveled a similar path. And guess what? They have much to offer us. And we have much to offer them as well. One thing we have in common with them is that we may have thought we were traveling our personal paths alone.

Yet so have they. It's not at all an uncommon characteristic of the human condition. But consider this: by the grace of God, we may well cross paths and connect with one of those fellow pilgrims if we keep our minds open to it. It may be at school or at our place of work. It may be in the person of a neighbor, a casual acquaintance, or someone for whom we have much respect. It may be a very close relative like a parent or a spouse, or it may be a friend, someone who doesn't yet realize that we are hurting, or who isn't sure how to approach us, what to say, or whether to say anything at all. It may be one or more people in a support group who can especially relate to our experiences, who care about our welfare, and who can make us realize we're not as different as we sometimes feel. Any one of them may well be ready and willing, even eager, to confide: "I know. I've been there. I, too, tried to run away. I, too, tried to hide. I, too, tried to escape my heartache and pain."

This connection may be just waiting to happen. When it does, our loneliness will diminish, and our fears will begin to subside. When at that surprising moment we realize that they, too, need us, when God-ordained circumstances topple a few of those walls we all tend to construct, something we never imagined could happen very well may—because we will have come face to face with someone who knows that he or she needs to be vulnerable. We may hear them share some of their most painful secrets. And as sure as the two of us are together in one place, we will immediately feel a most natural and compelling compassion. And we will offer them something they may not have felt for a long time—indeed, the very thing they have so longed for. We will offer them instant acceptance!

And now consider this: in the time it takes for new life to be conceived, they will offer and give us the same! Oh, to be sure, we may still long at times for that which ultimately cannot satisfy. We may still feel urges and temptations to take from others. We may still look for love and acceptance in all the wrong places. But we will also have found the very fulfillment for which we may have been desperately searching. We will have rediscovered the awesome, glorious, blessed joy of giving of ourselves to another.

If at this moment one of those people is not yet nearby, I invite you to read on, because we will find one of those people here. We'll meet a Bible character who clearly struggled to understand things that were happening in his life. Here we'll see an individual who found himself asking God, "Why me?" This is a man who wrestled with deep internal conflict, a man who knew what was right but sometimes found such things very hard to do. His name is Jonah.

Just as you and I sometimes have, Jonah also had a longing. Deep down he no doubt had a desire to be accepted, to be heard, to be loved unconditionally. As with me and maybe you, there were times when he searched for it in the wrong places, trying to meet those needs in the wrong ways. Like you and me, he knew that real love and acceptance could most fully be found in God. But like us to whatever degree, he, too, ignored that; he fled from the Lord. He fled as fast as he could in the other direction. But in time he discovered a blessed, wondrous reality. He learned that while he could run, he just couldn't find a way to hide.

These pages will take us into the short Old Testament Bible book that bears Jonah's name. The writer, while not explicitly identified, is widely regarded to be Jonah himself. Those who penned books of the Bible, including Jonah, were verbally inspired by its Divine Author. The Apostle Paul wrote, *"All Scripture is God-breathed" (2 Timothy 3:16).*

Jonah has a story to tell. I've got one, too, and I think you may have one as well. Some say we all have a story to tell. So I've decided to let Jonah tell you his story in the first person. I'll let him be the one to walk you through the brief Bible book he recorded, verse by verse, knowing all along what is very worth repeating, that ultimately it's not really his story. But, then, neither is mine. My own story is really the story of what my merciful God has done for me, in me, and through me, despite me. Perhaps that is true of you.

Letting Jonah speak to us in this way does of course mean speculating about what some of his thoughts could have been like, but third person accounts will often do the same. In the introduction to his insightful book *Called to Testify: The First Christian Witnesses*, Kenneth Kremer writes, "In first person accounts, we get a glimpse of our own stories. We inevitably conclude that the experiences of others are not so different from our own" (*Called to Testify*, Milwaukee: Northwestern Publishing House, 2003, p. vi.).

Our friend Jonah will speak of course from his perspective in time, a number of centuries before the birth of Jesus. I'll let him talk about that more specifically. But then as we let him guide us through his inspired account, we'll also let him step back a bit and with God's help and promised blessing adopt and adapt his wondrous Word to our own unique journey that he so graciously watches over and walks with us.

Jonah writes an account in which he is one of the main characters. In different ways and in varying degrees we may find ourselves identifying with this fascinating individual whose journey we will follow. Yet he would be the first to tell us that the account he recorded is ultimately not his story, not originating with him nor even primarily about him, though this Old Testament book of the Bible does bear his name.

No, we'll want to keep in mind that we will also be watching and hearing someone far more fascinating, for we will come face to face with someone who can fully meet the needs and desires of our hearts. It is my prayer that we will come to know a little better the One who provides those very friends, fellowships, and support systems of which we spoke.

He is the One who kept Jonah alive for three days in the belly of a great fish, and he is the One who can work miracles in our lives as well. He is the One who offers hope for our sometimes hurting hearts, meditation for our sometimes meandering minds, serenity for our sometimes struggling souls. He is the essence of giving. Let's meet here the One who will lead us to peace, to joy, and to a profound sense of personal fulfillment; the One who promises, *"Ask, and it will be given you; seek, and you will find; knock, and the door will be opened to you" (Matthew 7:7);* the One who is Love itself.

# - 1 -

# Calling

It was almost twenty-eight hundred years ago that God the Holy Spirit inspired me to write the Old Testament book of the Bible that bears my name. I am pleased for your interest in my personal story, but more importantly, a most dynamic lesson that God teaches in it. May God bless your journey through the fascinating book of Jonah.

**"The word of the LORD came to Jonah son of Amittai" (Jonah 1:1).** Excluding my father Amittai, my opening verse introduces you to two of the major characters in my historical account of the events I am about to unfold. Rest assured, we're going to let the Lord take center stage as we read the book he authored through my words. By comparison, I'm a minor character. Nevertheless, let me begin by telling you a little more about myself.

I am spoken of in only one other place in the Bible and that reference gives you a few facts about when and where I lived. In 2 Kings 14:25 the inspired writer Samuel tells how the Israelite king Jeroboam II restored the borders of Israel *"in accordance with the word of the LORD, the God of Israel, as spoken through his servant Jonah son of Amittai, the prophet from Gath Hepher."* My hometown was a tiny little village about three miles from

1

Nazareth, the little town where Jesus would eventually grow to manhood. That bit of information indicated that I spent my working years during the time of a king whose reign can be dated to the late 700's B.C.

In that verse Samuel also calls me a prophet. A prophet is someone who answers a call from God himself to serve as a public spokesperson for God, proclaiming God's Word and his will at his command and under his direction. A true prophet is one who is completely faithful to the Bible, speaking in strict accordance with it as the revelation of his Word to all people.

## My great privilege

You know, I was really a very fortunate man. I was someone who got a message from God himself. If ever I was lonely, if ever I wondered whether God was aware of my trials, or whether he would make his presence known in my life, I could consider myself blessed. Because God talked to me, and in the process he proved how very aware he was of me, my circumstances, and everything about me. It was very clear to me that all the events in every corner of the world, all the issues from the major to the mundane, and all the deeds being done, words being spoken, and thoughts bouncing around in every human mind were being monitored and managed around the clock. Simply put, not a one of these is ever a distraction for him.

The very first time God came to me was a calling. He came to me in his Word and promise of life. He called me out of the darkness of the unbelieving world, bringing me to faith in him and making me his child. That was all his doing. In his Word he promised to send me a Savior from my sin. And through that Word he filled my life with many more promises. What's more, I can't think of a single one that he ever broke. No, God didn't wait for me to come to him when he called me to faith. In fact, he was always the one who came calling to me, before

I came calling to him. He would always seek me out, before I sought him. That's why I wrote, *"The word of the LORD came to Jonah."*

But here's the thing. As a prophet, I've got to tell you this. God comes to you, too, and he hasn't stopped coming. God is as real in your life as a carpenter is to the house he built, as a surgeon is to the person whose life he saved, and as a caring, loving parent is to his or her child.

## Your call to faith

God is ultimately at the center of every story, isn't he? He is at the center of the book that bears my name as he is at the center of the Bible itself. And God and his grace are right at the center of the story of your life. He speaks to you, just as he spoke to me. Ultimately, what he reveals to us centers around the same blessed truth that he wants us to know and believe. He speaks of his Son Jesus, our Savior from our sins. The only difference is that he told me of the coming Savior, while he tells you of the Savior who has come. You have his full revelation, a completed Bible in both the Old Testament and the New.

It is in his Word that you will find the story of your own life told with the kind of truth and clarity that you could never know from any other source, including yourself. For it is there that the God who created you and knows you perfectly tells you the story of who you are, how much he loves you, what he has done for you, and what precious blessings you are destined to enjoy.

And while the entire Bible gives you that story in full, you can discover the story of God's unconditional love for you in the short little book of Jonah itself. This account that God moved me to write is only forty eight verses long. I encourage you to pick up a Bible at a time that works for you, look up this Old Testament book, and read it through in its entirety.

## Your call has a purpose

Many intelligent people in your time have been hoodwinked into believing in the theory of evolution. Atheistic evolution ultimately tries to convince people that they are masters of their own fate, and it leaves them no hope. Others believe in a variation called theistic evolution, grasping at a compromise theory of their origin. The idea here is that there is a God who created the world's raw materials, but then like a child who fires up a gyroscope or pumps up one of those spinning top toys from the past, God let the universe evolve on its own. This bundle of confusion leaves people all alone and utterly detached from a God too big and busy to be bothered by their business.

But God made all things for a purpose. He created human beings whom he could love and who could live with him in a blessed fellowship and love him faithfully in return. When we failed and severed that awesome relationship we had with him, he came to us in person. Jesus came to us in perfect, self-sacrificing love to save us for eternity. He gave us his life. He took our sin and every bit of our shame onto himself. He carried a cross laid on him and was crucified in our place.

He saved us *from* sin and hell. He saved us *for* a restored relationship and to once again experience living and loving. He saved us *for* the joy of giving and serving and making a blessed impact in his world. He made us *for* a purpose. And through faith in him, created and strengthened by his Spirit, he made us his children with a purpose, that you and I might *"declare the praises of him who called you out of darkness and into his marvelous light" (I Peter 2:9).*

There's absolutely no doubt about it—God does think that highly of you! At this very moment you are the one he is calling. In the same way that God had an ongoing mission and purpose in mind for me, so God has an ongoing purpose for your life and sets it before you on an ongoing basis, a purpose that ultimately has to do with other people.

## Your call is to service

Yes, you are the one he has in mind for a most noble cause and purpose. It may be a continuing call, one that you have engaged in for some time. Or it may be something newer. At its heart and core it is a spiritual calling. God calls you to faith through his gospel; his Spirit works that faith in you. At the same time God calls you to service, which flows naturally from your faith.

The heart that has come to believe in the Savior is one that has a new relationship with him. It is a heart that is filled with gratitude and love. It is a heart that regards God now with awe and reverence, one that hears his life giving promises and learns to lean on them with hope, trust, and joy. These characteristics of the heart are created, nurtured, and grown in you by the same Spirit who breathed spiritual life in you for the first time. In Galatians 5:22 Paul uses the imagery of a plant, a vine, or a tree that produces fruit: *"The fruit of the Spirit is love, joy, peace, goodness, kindness, gentleness, and self-control."*

As God calls us to service, his gospel empowers us and motivates us to serve him. He gave us a moral compass through his natural law that was written on our hearts, but because that natural law was clouded by sin, it is the moral law written in his Word that gives clarity to issues of right and wrong. Beyond that, God has given us an abundance of Christian freedom to make our life choices in matters that he has not specifically commanded or forbidden. In his Word he has so much to teach us as we seek out his will for our lives. It gives us guiding principles. It teaches us, for example, *"Love the LORD your God with all your heart and with all your soul and with all your mind,"* and *"Love your neighbor as yourself"* (Matthew 22:37,38). Jesus said, for example, *"Love your enemies, and pray for those who persecute you"* (Matthew 5:44). So it is that in calling us to faith, he simultaneously calls us to simply serve him to the best of our ability.

As he calls us through his Word, it is there that he promises much. He promises to be with us every step of the way. He promises to help us. He promises to make all things work out for the best for us.

Listen to him calling to you in his Word. Discover there his will for your life. Seek and you will find.

You see, this is the very way that the God of love came to me. All my life he was teaching me through his Word. Then one day he spoke to me directly, calling me to serve him in a specific way as a spokesman, or prophet. God originally called me to prophesy to my fellow Israelites, the people whom he chose to carry the promise of the Savior, who would be born among them. Do you remember how II Kings 14:25 pointed out that the Israelite king expanded Israel's borders in accordance with the word of the Lord that I spoke to him? He blessed my work with a certain kind of success. The nation and its king listened to God's message that I proclaimed, and they were strengthened. The Lord of love had a purpose for my life, and in keeping with that will and purpose he gave me that commission.

## My new call

This is significant because one day, like a bolt out of the blue, I was called by God to proclaim his Word somewhere else. And what an amazing call it was! The book of Jonah relates the account of how God called me to serve him temporarily in a new way, as a missionary to the people of Assyria, a nation that was Israel's, and therefore my own worst enemy.

Now by my way of thinking at the time, that nation should have been God's worst enemy as well. I'm not going to pretend it was very clearheaded thinking on my part, but I have to be honest with you. That was my mindset.

But the word of the Lord came to me as it had come to me in the past. Just as before, it was a most holy event. You see, *"the word of the LORD"* is the revelation of God's grace, his totally undeserved love, his full, free, and completely unmerited favor. Love came to me. He took me up in his arms.

God had come to me with glorious life opportunities, but now he came to me again with that amazing new commission: **"Go to the great city of Nineveh and preach against it, because its wickedness has come up before me" (1:2).**

"Stop what you're doing, Jonah, and listen," he was saying to me. "There's something I want you to do, somewhere I want you to go. I have a job for you. I have a mission I need someone to carry out—in fact, a great and glorious and most rewarding mission—and Jonah, you're the man."

Go! "Go to the great city of Nineveh!" Go, right now, to the great capital city of the most powerful nation on earth! God wanted me to not dwell on whatever feelings I might have had, because he knew what was best for all concerned. He wanted me to forget about waiting for the right feelings to come along. He wanted me to just act, because he knew that in time the feelings would follow. You may know that to preach is to proclaim a message. I was to go to that big city and confront its many inhabitants.

This was something very different. Now he was calling me to go directly to the major metropolis of Nineveh and to preach against it. Essentially, my message to the people of Nineveh was not going to be substantially different from the message I proclaimed to the people of Israel. Nineveh's wickedness had not gone unseen. Nineveh needed to hear that its wickedness would not go unpunished. Someone needed to talk to these people. They needed to be convicted of their sins, for they lived with the false security that their wicked sins were no big deal. In their personal lives, they had concluded that they were accountable to no one but themselves and could follow whatever self-centered sinful inclination they pleased. They needed to be dethroned so that God could be enthroned in his rightful place in their hearts and lives.

When that happened, when they would be brought to the point of despair, God would give them hope through the full and free forgiveness of the gospel that I would then proclaim. Believe me, I consider myself richly blessed to have had the high privilege of being an ambassador of the great news of Jesus' coming. Regardless of how my message would be received, mine would be the voice of truth. I would be God's instrument for saving souls. What a calling it was! What a calling it would be to save even one life, and not only for this life, but for eternity!

# - 2 -

# Flight

"But Jonah ran away from the LORD and headed for Tarshish. He went down to Joppa, where he found a ship bound for that port. After paying the fare, he went aboard and sailed for Tarshish to flee from the LORD" (1:3).

Whoa, now there's a surprise! "Not so fast," I said to the Lord. "I'm not going there! Not me!"

You see, I did not agree with God's plan for me. I did not want to go to Nineveh to preach against its inhabitants and their wickedness. I refused to do it. It's not the most flattering chapter of my life, but it's the one God wants you to know about.

So that's right, I turned and headed in the opposite direction. I didn't walk, I ran! Not to the Lord, but away from him. I headed straight for Joppa, the nearest sea port, looking for a ship that was ready to sail! "Call me an average Joe," I said, "call me Jo to Go, but this is a career change, and it's happening now!" In the original Hebrew language that I spoke and wrote, the idea that my words convey is that I fled from "the presence of the Lord."

9

I bet I know what you're thinking. If God is everywhere, how can a person flee from his presence? Good point! I'm not sure if I can conceive of a more futile exercise myself! But, of course, kids who run away from home aren't the only people who try to escape from their problems. I think that most of us have a way of doing that as a way of life to some degree.

*Modern Tel Aviv/Jaffa, the general vicinity where
Jonah boarded a ship in his flight from the Lord.*

But don't let that get you down. Stay with me on this, because if you are anything like me, if your life story has any resemblance at all to mine, then I hope and pray that you never give up or give in to despair. You see, even though I did a bad thing, God didn't badger me, scold me, chastise me, or punish me in any way whatsoever. In fact, he just loved me all the more.

So, hear me out! Let's explore more closely the concept of running away from God. Let's do so boldly, because with God, truth is always surrounded by his compassionate love. Let truth hurt a bit if it may, but know that it is the path to healing and peace. Let's walk this path together, one step at a time.

## Our natural inclination

You see, already in our mother's womb, from the time we were conceived, we were tainted and corrupted by sin. That sinful nature severed our relationship with our Creator even as we were being "knit together" (Psalm 51:5) and shaped in our earliest biological stages of development. Jesus said, *"Flesh gives birth to flesh" (John 3:6a).* The sinful nature gives birth to the sinful nature.

Humanity became morally imperfect as soon as Adam and Eve committed their first sins. Their jealous son Cain murdered his only sibling, his brother Abel. We call this sinful nature "inherited sin." No two sinners can produce a perfect, holy child. Were that the case, then, environment notwithstanding, one could wonder why such holiness could not be retained. How quickly this world would improve!

But the truth is it's in our very nature to sin against God. *"The sinful mind is hostile to God" (Romans 8:7).* We are "rebels without a cause." We might test this truth in this way. Reflect on the past two hours. In your thoughts, words, or actions over the past two hours, whose interests did you serve the most? Those of a helpless infant? An impoverished child? A victim of harsh trauma well beyond anything we've experienced? A third degree burn victim? Actually, in the last two hours you and I may not have even realized that we had decided to do something nice for someone, and that someone was you and me. It was automatic.

It is true that we do that for others too, caring about their needs without giving it a thought. We are sometimes just as passionate about serving God. We may love God or loved ones just as intensely.

Nevertheless our personal record is clear. Every minute of every day we think first and most naturally in terms of our own desires first.

Often what God wants is not what we want. We choose what we want. We are not in harmony with God's will. His will is revealed in his Word, but we disobey it. Every day we break the first commandment, *"You shall have no other gods before me," (Exodus 20:3)*. Why do I say that? Because anything or anyone put ahead of God at any given moment is a god, a false god, something or someone not God that is set in his place, occupying the place in our hearts and minds that rightly belongs to him alone.

We become guilty of doing the opposite of what God tells us, like I did. We go in the opposite direction. We run the other way.

## My stubborn resistance

Run the other way? Did I ever! But why? Why did I not want to go to Nineveh to preach against its inhabitants? Your first thought might be that I harbored an understandable fear of confrontation. I was, after all, asked to go to the city alone, a stranger to them, to challenge them and to take issue with things they were doing, in fact how they lived their lives. You're right if you're thinking this would be intensely personal. I was to accuse them of wrongdoing in every area of their lives. I was to command them to give up things they loved the most. I was to inform them that God recognized them as guilty and that the only possible right sentence was to perish in hell. God's perfect justice demanded it.

But I have to tell you, this is not something I was afraid to do. Because I, too, believed that is what the people of Nineveh deserved. The problem was that I seem to have been thinking they deserved it more than I did, and more than my fellow Israelites did. Nineveh was the capital city of Assyria, and Assyria was the brutal empire that, as it turns out, would one day carry our Israelite nation away into captivity. You see, while God granted Israel outward success when their borders were expanded, nevertheless, they became very complacent and in time abandoned God completely.

That was very discouraging to me to say the least, and I was aware of the prophecies that God was eventually going to use a foreign power to bring judgment on his people who refused to repent of their rebellious ways and ultimate rejection of him. I cared deeply for my people. But that doesn't mean that I shouldn't have cared equally for all people, including the people of that nation that were an enemy of my people! If I was a public servant and ambassador of my Lord, that obviously should have been my mindset.

I knew that the message I was to proclaim was not only that of God's justice, it was also a message of God's grace, his perfect love in his Son, the coming Savior. At the heart and core of every prophetic message that I proclaimed was God's promise to save all people of every nation of all time. The message of his justice, and the message of his grace—they are the two main teachings of God's Word, the key to understanding the entire Bible, and the key to life itself. We call them law and gospel, and they are God's revelation to you as well.

But let's explore that a little more fully. Telling us that we have sinned is God's first order of business. Only when we are aware of our sins can we be sorry for them. The first part of God's message is that we owe him an apology. It is critical for him to communicate that truth, for how else can a person correct his way? The knowledge of the gravity of our sin shatters our sinful pride and brings us to our knees in despair.

And then we are open to hearing the glorious message of forgiveness in our Savior Jesus. It is the central truth of the Scriptures. That wondrous gospel that brings such joy to the world is the predominant message that will permeate the remaining chapters of the book of Jonah. For the moment, just listen to a few of those awesome biblical proclamations of the Great News:

> *"God so loved the world that he gave his one and only Son, that whoever believes in him will not perish, but have everlasting life" (John 3:16).*

> *"The Son of Man did not come to be served, but to serve, and to give his life as a ransom for many" (Matthew 20:28).*

> *"He was pierced for our transgression, he was crushed for our iniquities; the punishment that brought us peace was upon him, and by his wounds we are healed" (Isaiah 53:5).*

> *"God made him who had no sin to be sin for us, so that in him we might become the righteousness of God" (2 Corinthians 5:21).*

> *"Christ redeemed us from the curse of the law by becoming a curse for us" (Galatians 3:13).*

> *"There is now no condemnation for those who are in Christ Jesus" (Romans 8:1).*

> *"It is by grace you are saved, through faith—and this not from yourselves, it is the gift of God—not by works, so that no one will boast" (Ephesians 2:8,9).*

> *"I am the resurrection and the life. He who believes in me will live, even though he dies; and whoever lives and believes in me will never die" (John 11:25,26).*

Oh, and there are so many more! What joy, what certain hope, what peace we have in Jesus!

## I try to hide

Yes, the very heart of my calling as a prophet was this wonderful opportunity to save people from hell by telling them of a coming Messiah, a Savior from their sins, and calling them to faith in him.

So why didn't I want to go to Nineveh to preach against the Assyrian people? I was human. I had trouble feeling good about God letting the brutal Assyrian people off the hook so easily. I had been tempted to despise these enemies of his people, and I had yielded to that temptation. This may be hard to understand, but maybe the best way to explain it is that I wanted the brutal regime destroyed, not saved and preserved so that it could remain not only a threat to my nation's security but a threat to our very existence!

Yet I should have entrusted my country to the care of its Creator and Redeemer! Hung up on that sin, I had trouble letting go of it. I harbored it because there was a payback in it for me. I think maybe the brutality of that bullying nation was just eating away at me. I know it aroused such anger in me that I found soothing and escape from my frustration in the fact that these murdering hordes could not escape justice forever, that they would one day have to account for their deeds—if not in this world, then in the next.

I resisted God's plan and purpose for me in calling Nineveh to repentance and faith in his full and free forgiveness in Jesus. I could not bring myself to love these people at all, much less with the passionate intensity of God's grace. I didn't want to be smiling at them and being their friend any more than you would have wanted to befriend the commanding officers of Adolph Hitler. What bothered me the most was the simple fact that I would be helping the enemy.

I had been counting on God to free my people from our enemy, not to deliver us into their hands. If the Ninevites repented of their sin, they would be saved, and as I said, by my reckoning, they would remain in power and my fellow citizens would suffer the consequences. The critical fact to which I let myself be blinded was that all my people needed to do was to repent of their wickedness and turn to their God, and they would most certainly be spared!

So despite the fact that this awesome calling made me the most privileged person on the planet, this was not a mission I would accept. My answer to God was "No way!" Then I solidified my answer by simply traveling away from the people of Nineveh as far as I could go. I figured I could hardly do this thing God had in mind if I was thousands of miles away from that place where I would have to be.

By trying to escape this mission, I was in reality trying to escape from God. I ran away from God as though I could hide from him. But I guess we all know that isn't going to happen. Any attempt to escape God's will for our lives is going to be futile. I ran, but I couldn't hide.

But I tried. I fled. I ran away from the Lord. My destination was a city called Tarshish. You want to know why I picked that city? Because Tarshish was about as far away as a man could get. While Nineveh was about six hundred miles northeast, not all that far from your present day Baghdad in Iraq, Tarshish was some two thousand miles to the west, on the opposite end of the Mediterranean Sea. "Go west, young man" was all I wanted to do. "Tarshish or Bust" was my slogan, which was actually rather prophetic in itself. Finding a ship bound for Tarshish was like you grabbing a one-way flight to Australia. It would take me a long, long time to get there, and even if I had a change of heart or God came calling again, it would take a long, long time to get back. I wanted to sabotage that idea in advance

Yes, I fled. I fled from God to a ship, which promptly sailed right into his hands.

# - 3 -

# Intervention

**"T**hen the LORD sent a great wind on the sea, and such a violent storm arose that the ship threatened to break up" (1:4).**

Into the hands of God indeed! My headstrong, headlong flight from the Lord now came to a screeching halt. A "great wind" came up on the sea. This "violent storm" is one that "the Lord sent." It was kind of like a scene from some of those movies you people have—a man running away full speed, looking over his shoulder, only to run headlong into the person he's fleeing!

The storm sent by God was so violent that the ship was in danger of breaking up. It was brutal out there. The raging power of the tempest terrified every hand on deck. **"All the sailors were afraid and each cried out to his own god" (1:5a).**

When a crisis strikes full force, where does one turn? To a man, every one of these sailors made the same choice. It was the only choice they knew. They turned to their man-made gods. But you might be wondering why. What made that such an obvious thing for them to do?

That's a fair question, as I see it. The answer is, it is such a universal choice that you and I will realize that we have made the same mistake, and to our own amazement, we'll acknowledge that we have done so repeatedly. You see, a god, a false god, is anything or anyone held dearer than God in one's heart. It is that which one considers most powerful and important, that which one considers most highly, that which one turns to first for help.

It would be nice to be able to say that we have managed to keep God's first commandment which forbids the worship of false gods. But we can't. For we too have so often been inclined to flee problems by reaching for help from a god of our own making, blindly believing we had no other choice because we thought we were finding what we needed. Our idols, of course, never helped at all.

Neither did the false gods of the sailors, like Baal, the god of rain and thunder. When turning to them didn't work, the men started to come to their senses and finally began to focus on some reasonable crisis management. **"And they threw the cargo into the sea to lighten the ship" (1:5b).** It was time to cut their losses to save their lives. Still, the gale force winds blew and shipwreck seemed imminent.

## My wakeup call

Let's recap for a moment. I was in full headlong flight from the Lord. By definition, that made it nothing less than a spiritual flight. To the point, I was in danger of committing spiritual suicide. This, however, my gracious God would not allow without a fight.

Maybe you've been getting the idea that it was me whom the Lord was reaching out to with this raging storm on the sea. Well, I think you're onto something! This was no less than divine intervention, with the threat of a natural disaster being the Master's instrument. But now, take note. As God intervened (and quite loudly if I may say so), did his loving hand stop me in my tracks? Let's take a look.

**"But Jonah had gone below deck, where he lay down and fell into a deep sleep" (1:5c).** What's this? I was sleeping? With everyone else running about, terrified for their lives? The ship's captain wondered the same thing!

**"The captain went to him and said, 'How can you sleep?'" (1: 6a).** Did God's intervention have its desired effect, that is to say, did I now come to my senses? Well, let's put it this way: not yet.

**"The captain continued, 'Get up and call on your god. Maybe he will take note of us, and we will not perish'" (1:6b).** Sometimes God uses the most fascinating ways to intervene in our lives. That sure was the case here, wasn't it? Out of his toolbox he pulls another instrument of intervention—the heathen captain, who had far more common sense going for him in this crisis than the man so privileged to have God speaking to him so directly.

The captain knew that I was a prophet of some kind. "What in blazes are you doing down here, man? Wake up and start calling on your god!" I mean, if ever there was a time to throw up a prayer to God, wouldn't this be one of those times? Clearly something was amiss! I'm telling you, this was more than a physical sleep I was in; it was a spiritual slumber as well. Wouldn't you expect me of all people to have been praying all along? After all, wasn't that my job? I mean, really, if as a prophet I was any kind of spokesman for God, wouldn't I have to be in pretty close communication with him?

Of course. But this was full scale flight, one of those "throw in the towel" times that make no sense at all. It was a complete abdication of my responsibility. I had very effectively tuned God out. And in such a spiritual vacuum the idol of self will always be erected. It's no wonder I wasn't answering God's calls. I wasn't about to pick up the phone! I was screening my calls and filtering out all God messages!

Have you ever noticed that when you start to build a wall between you and God, you are often building walls between you and others? It is as though you just want to hide. I seemed to be hiding from anyone and everyone who might begin wondering out loud what in heaven's name I was doing. Without divine intervention, the meandering mind and the struggling soul will slowly lose touch with reality. Eventually the thinking is so distorted it approaches full blown insanity.

You know, that was some pretty significant embarrassment I was feeling while the captain was so rightly berating me. Not a pleasant feeling, but I was masking a fair amount of inner shame. And God in his grace and wisdom knew that had to be faced head on.

I didn't relate to you whether or not I prayed at this point yet. The Spirit did not move me to share that. But you do get a sense that at least I might have been starting to wake up a little.

*A fishing boat roams the waters of the Mediterranean Sea in Greece, a few hundred miles from the port where Jonah set out to sea.*

## My comrades react

Nevertheless, the heathen sailors were still way ahead of me. They were exhausted from struggling at the oars of that ancient vessel to no avail. They'd been hard at it, trying everything they could think of. But they never gave up, this hardy bunch. Good thing, too, seeing as there wasn't a whole lot of time to spare.

Used to thinking on their feet, now they had an idea. **"Then the sailors said to each other, 'Come let us cast lots and see who is responsible for this calamity"** (1:7a). This statement was very revealing. First of all, they came to a common conclusion about their distressing situation. They came to believe that someone was responsible.

Someone responsible for an act of God? That may sound foreign to your ears. But the truth is, they were definitely onto something, weren't they? You and I know why the storm was there. And if some Higher Power was after someone, they could at least try to find out who it was that the deity was looking to corner, or maybe even exterminate.

So the consensus was that they should cast lots in order to pinpoint responsibility. Casting lots was a common practice by which many people sought the will of their gods. It happened to also be sometimes used by those who believed in the true God, in matters where he hadn't given direction and where a question was unsettled. Occasionally God commanded its use in certain matters of great importance. There were different kinds of lots, such as small round pebbles or pieces of wood. They were cast in a random way into a circle drawn on the ground or into or out of a container, and by processes of elimination, decisions could be made. Maybe you've played a board game with three other people and you throw dice to decide who goes first, second, third, and last. Since God controls all things, you might say you were letting him decide the order.

**"They cast lots and the lots fell on Jonah" (1:7b).** God was directing these events. With amazing love, he continued to reach out to me, his wayward prophet. Maybe I started to feel God closing in on me at that point. More likely, I think I was recognizing his parental hand reaching out with a gentle touch. I knew God, and I heard his gentle whisper in the midst of the raging tempest.

To be sure, I was reminded that a man can run all he wants, but he can never hide. Perhaps you've heard the words of the Psalmist:

> *"Where can I go from your Spirit?*
> *Where can I flee from your presence?*
> *If I go up to the heavens, you are there,*
> *if I make my bed in the depths, you are there.*
> *If I rise on the wings of the dawn,*
> *if I settle on the far side of the sea,*
> *even there your hand will guide me,*
> *your right hand will hold me fast" (Psalm 139:7-12).*

# - 4 -

# Recovery

The sailors considered death imminent. Maybe some of them were seeing their lives flash before their eyes. They were familiar with the many gods that were worshiped in their day, but they'd never seen power like this before. That should come as no surprise, because they'd never witnessed anything supernatural before and the magnanimity of this went beyond what the laws of nature would ordinarily produce. There were no atheists on this ship. They were definitely approaching the subject with an open mind.

The lots had fallen on me. **"So they asked him, 'Tell us, who is responsible for making all this trouble for us? What do you do? Where do you come from? What is your country? From what people are you?'" (1:8).** You can probably picture them surrounding me, shouting all sorts of questions at once. To all the questions about who I was, I answered simply, **"I am a Hebrew."** To the question of what I did, I continued, **"And I worship the LORD, the God of heaven, who made the sea and the land" (1:9).**

The sailors had already heard me mention my God. In the following verse, you'll see that I had already told them that I was fleeing the Lord.

I suppose they fairly well shrugged at that. What was surprising about a man afraid of one of his gods? It's actually an illustration of what is called natural religion because such thinking is a typical product of our anthropocentric, or human-centered, way of thinking. It is completely natural for us to think that when it comes to religion and all matters spiritual, it's all about behaving. It's all about being a good person. In fact, it's all about being good enough to please God, which, if one carries this through logically, should have the effect of stark terror. If human punishment has at time been far beyond horrific, imagine what punishment from God could be like!

## God's truth revealed

But in my brief answer to their simple questions, I was really giving them a much fuller picture of God. I called him "the God of heaven, who made the sea and the land." Already this was saying a great deal. My description of God already went way beyond what they generally associated with a god. They were used to gods who could never be that all-encompassing.

Likely you're more familiar with the respective Greek and Roman mythology that came about a few centuries after my time. You'll remember Zeus and Jupiter, their god of sky and thunder, Hermes and Mercury, their messenger god, Aphrodite and Venus, their goddess of love, and so on. In my day the same kind of polytheism prevailed. The sailors had been desperately crying out to their Phoenician gods. They had quite a selection—Baal, their god of rain and thunder, Melgart their god of the sea, Esmus their god of ships and sailing, and many more.

But the God I spoke of sounded like one mighty Ruler of everything. In specifying that God made the sea and the land, I was making the connection that the imminent desperate situation demanded. Yes, it was my God who was doing this. But I'm sure it was clear from my succinct words that this was not a god who was summoning every bit of supernatural strength he had and unleashing it with all the fury he could muster. This was the only God there is, and while he was the One behind this mighty squall, he was also very much in control of it, because he ruled all things. This was nothing but a puff of his nostril, and you can be sure, it wouldn't be hard for him to make it a whole lot worse. (I wasn't about to let them in on the fact that God at one time had carried out his perfect justice with a Flood that deluged the whole earth.)

Oh, to be on the side of divine truth! What an incredible privilege to be recipients of divine revelation! How awesome that God has chosen to tell us about himself and, by the power of his Spirit, to lead us to believe it! Still sleepy, I answered a simple question, and in so doing taught these sailors more than they had ever known. David in one of his Psalms says, *"The fear of the LORD is the beginning of wisdom" (Psalm 111:10).* The kind of fear David is referring to is not terror, but child like awe and wonder that comes from knowing the all-powerful God who is Love itself.

## A God of grace and mercy

That takes us back to my simple answer, because we left out the most important thing. I had not only used the name "God" which emphasizes our Creator's power; I said, "I worship the LORD." Hearing me in the Hebrew language I spoke, the sailors were introduced to "Yahweh." It is a most special name for God, because its meaning goes beyond a reference to his power, and speaks to us of his grace, that is, the perfect love he showers on us that is fully and completely undeserved. Your New International Version of the Bible that we're using here calls attention to this by using the upper case letters. In Exodus 34:6,7 God defines his own name: *"The LORD, the LORD, the compassionate and gracious God, slow to anger, abounding in love and faithfulness, maintaining love to thousands and forgiving wickedness, rebellion and sin. Yet he will not leave the guilty unpunished…"* While this name refers to God's twin attributes of perfect justice and perfect love, the emphasis is on his love.

Listen to the piling up of comforting attributes used to describe the Lord in these two verse: gracious, compassionate, patient, loving richly, forever faithful, forgiving, merciful. He is all this to all people, for he sent Jesus to the world to pay for the sins of all. When the passage says he shows mercy to thousands who love him and obey his commands, it is speaking specifically of those who receive him by faith, contrasting with those who do not, and who are spoken of in the words that follow. By definition, a Christian is one who loves him and obeys his commands—not perfectly by any means, but he or she still does so, because it is a natural product of Spirit-worked faith in Jesus. The passage is saying that those who believe in him by the power of that Spirit are the recipients of that full and free forgiveness.

If you came to know the Lord from early on, you can consider that one of your greatest blessings. Proverbs 22:6 says, *"Train up a child in the way of the LORD, and when he is old, he will not depart from it."* With early nurture and regular reinforcement, your roots ran deep. And so in your most critical moments, God was there, and you knew him.

Likewise, at the most critical moment in the pressure cooker of that crisis off the Mediterranean coast, it was very easy for me to say, "I worship the Lord, the God of heaven, who made the sea and the land." I could have professed that truth in my sleep.

My simple answer that revealed the identity of the Lord to my comrades felt like a thunderbolt to them. **"This terrified them and they asked, 'What have you done?' (They knew he was running away from the LORD, because he had already told them so)" (1:10).**

## The crisis in perspective

A new stage in this episode was setting in. For both the sailors and for me this was a reality check. Prior to this, the sailors were swirling around in the middle of turmoil. Turned upside down physically, mentally, and emotionally, they had no idea what hit them. They couldn't help but be totally out of touch with what was really going on. And I had most certainly been lost in my own world.

But my twenty word confession of faith finally put everything into perspective. That's what happens when one puts Truth on the table. And when the true God is put in his rightful place in the center of whatever scene or situation is involved, order starts coming out of chaos again.

True, the minds of skeptics and doubters may suddenly be sent scurrying as their proverbial boats are rocked, but that is a very good thing. When the conversation starts to include God and his truths, things start getting right again.

The reality check left the men stunned and shell-shocked, but at least now they knew what they were facing. Now real crisis management could begin. Finally they knew what direction to go, because it was no longer all the logical attempts to save a ship at peril. The emergency plan had been rewritten, and it was most simple: find out from the true God's prophet what they should do.

**"The sea was getting rougher and rougher. So they asked him, 'What should we do to make the sea calm down for us?'" (1:11).**

Things were getting overwhelming for me to say the least, but the crisis that was imminent was an impending catastrophe threatening both body and soul. Like the sailors, I stood face to face with reality. No longer could I get away with my denial. The truths I had been denying included the fact that I had been wrong all along, that I should have heeded God's calling in the first place, that this stormy weather was probably an issue to be dealt with, that this crisis was a consequence of my own choices, and that it was well past time to wake up!

And awake I finally was. The Lord had tapped me on the shoulder and had successfully gotten my full attention. He now laid on me the heaviest responsibility of my life. Transformed, I stepped up to the plate and delivered. Though I was not led to explicitly state it in the book of Jonah, truly the Spirit of the Lord came on me with power.

Gone was the complainer. Back again was the Lord's servant. You can imagine the full gamut of emotions I felt in the brief time it took for these events to unfold. But when the most critical moment of truth came, there stood a warrior for the Lord ready to take my blows like a man, a redeemed child of God willing even to sacrifice my life on behalf of those endangered men. My recovery was underway.

## I am but a servant

**"Pick me up and throw me into the sea," he replied, "and it will become calm. I know that it is my fault that this great storm has come upon you" (1:12).**

I was contrite. I freely confessed my sin, but without despairing of it. Judas was one who despaired after his contrition. But despair doesn't keep the Creator enthroned where the Creator belongs, because it refuses to accept the invitation to faith and forgiveness that is so freely offered. I knew the Lord. I knew his forgiveness in the promised Messiah covered the most treacherous of sins, and without hesitation I embraced it. My willingness to die was a fruit of repentance. I recognized it as the consequence that my rebellious flight had produced, the impending calamity that I had brought on the whole lot of them. This is the essence of faith. A repentant heart that is first contrite, but secondly one that accepts the payment for sin that is offered at a price—the holy, precious blood of the Savior who was to come, and his innocent suffering and death.

How was I so sure that it was God's will for me to be thrown overboard? God revealed that to me in a supernatural way, just as he revealed to me my calling and message. This was how God spoke to his people in the days before the Holy Bible was fully revealed in the complete Old Testament and in the New.

Just as it was God's will that I should be facing death in order to save the entire crew of the ship, so it was his will that one day his own Son would be facing death to save the entire human race. Just as the result of my sacrifice would be an immediate calm and serenity for those struggling sailors, so the result of Jesus' sacrifice would be an immediate calm and serenity for every struggling soul.

The parallels will not be perfect however, because my impending substitutionary death would be a consequence of my own sin, and my sacrifice would only give my shipmates a temporary respite from the death they would all one day experience. Jesus' death, on the other hand, was a true substitution, a ransom payment that actually did satisfy the justice of God, and brought real deliverance from death for both body and soul.

But the men in the boat were not the kind of ragged ruffians one might see depicted in some movie plot set in these ancient times. Rugged looking they might have been, but in this incident recorded for the benefit of all humanity they displayed nothing but the highest virtue and character. It most certainly may have been an immediate result of their newborn faith. In the midst of their peril they had discovered what they knew to be the kind of Truth that was the answer to the most critical questions faced by every human being. Through the singular words of a prophet, every deep and nagging doubt of their souls disappeared. They had come face to face with the one Creator who clearly had the power and right to punish, but whom they were hearing desired to save them.

They heard and believed that my death would give them life. But faith is a relationship, and from faith flows love. Even the kind of brotherly love for a stranger, or an enemy. Now it was their turn, and at further peril to their own lives, they were not ready to toss a man overboard. After all, they couldn't read God's mind perfectly, and the courage they displayed all along was only stoked all the more. If they could help it, they would yet save the man who was ready to die for them.

**"Instead the men did their best to row back to land" (1:13a).** This sea was like a giant flaming balrog, but now they were stirred, and if they were put on this planet for a purpose, as they now sensed they were, well then, by God, they were going to fulfill their destiny. They were going to tame this wild beast; they were going to stare this storm down. Most merchant vessels in those days remained within sight of the shore, and it seems likely as well that God didn't let the ship get too far on its voyage before he intervened. They tried desperately to reach land.

## Providence with a purpose

But alas, to no avail. God surely must have smiled. That mankind should display such virtuous love was the reason for its creation. He was pleased with the well meaning actions that were products of faith. Yet he steered the course of events to accomplish a greater good, one that would become amply clear for the sake of all posterity. **"But they could not, for the sea grew even wilder than before" (1:13b).**

And so it all came back to their Higher Power. Any power greater than yourself can potentially help you, if it is so inclined or steered. A friend with good advice, the protective arm of a parent, a doctor and nurse, your soldiers overseas, a government agency or community program that is people helping people. But *every good and perfect gift is from above, and comes down from the Father of heavenly lights" (James 1:17)*. There is only one who can save body and soul from death. Ultimately, there is only one Higher Power.

No human power had been available to the sailors, and so they had turned desperately to their own manufactured gods, frantically pleading in prayer for help. But not any more—now they knew they might as well have been talking to a tree. Now they turned to God. But their level of fear was inversely proportional to the level of danger they faced. As the storm's fury increased, their panic diminished. The more intensely the waves and sheets of rain crashed over them, the more calm and serene they were. Like a child huddled to the bosom of its mother oblivious to all the destruction of a tornado's aftermath, the men calmly addressed their Father in heaven. They may have had to raise their voices above the howling winds, but within them where it counted lay trusting hearts.

**"Then they cried to the LORD, 'Oh, please do not let us die for taking this man's life. Do not hold us accountable for killing an innocent man, for you, O LORD, have done as you pleased.' Then they took Jonah and threw him overboard, and the raging sea grew calm" (1:14,15).**

The sailors understood that I was guilty before God, but to them I was "innocent" in that I hadn't meant to do them harm. Throwing me overboard was not what they wanted to do. But in the end they realized they had no choice, for God had settled the matter. I was flung into the foaming waves, a God-pleasing scapegoat, and the sea was stilled.

## Calmed seas, calmed hearts

**"At this the men greatly feared the LORD, and they offered a sacrifice to the LORD and made vows to him" (1:16).** Your Bible, in its original languages, has more than one word for your word "fear." Terror in the face of his power and threat of punishment was not this kind of fear. Here it means an awe of him and high respect for him. This fear flows from faith, a certain knowledge of his nature as a God of perfect love and an intense desire to save every soul. The sacrifice these men offered him was something of value aboard the ship, presented to him in heartfelt gratitude. They vowed to serve him only from this point on.

God is at the center of this account, and he is worthy of all praise. We witnessed his great power. And you may think I'm speaking of his stirring up great storms, but we saw a far greater demonstration of his power, didn't we? Indeed, the conversion of these men.

I'm sure these men were people you would have enjoyed meeting if you lived then. In many ways you could identify with them, I'm sure, but in the introduction of this book the hope was also expressed that you would identify with me. You see, I think there is something very encouraging here. It was my simple witness of the Lord that brought these people to faith. And did that occur through my powerful preaching and stellar life? Hardly! So what does this mean for you?

God can most certainly use you! He can accomplish great and mighty things through you even when you consider your efforts to be feeble at best. "I haven't set a very good example," you may feel. But is that not in the past?

Hasn't God said, *"I will remember their sins no more" (Jeremiah 31:34).* And along with me here, did he not powerfully use the gospel writer Matthew, who was a despised tax collector when he was called? Didn't Jesus commission Peter, after Peter three times heatedly denied even knowing him? Didn't he single out Paul in the middle of his ferocious attempts to stamp out Christianity and move him to be a fearless missionary to the Gentile world? He did not dethrone David as king of Israel after his sins of adultery and murder. He continued to reach out to Solomon after he began chasing all the vain pleasures of life. Eve taught her progeny about the promise of the Savior, as did Adam, after they brought sin into this world, and we have that promise and know our Savior because they did so. The biblical examples go on and on.

In the midst of my shame, I spoke twenty words, and they dramatically changed the fortunes of these men. My words brought them life.

# - 5 -

# Prayer

B ut wait a minute. You've probably been waiting for me to return to the story, since it left me floundering in the water. The way we've been talking, you could certainly be excused for presuming me dead. Oh, there have been great stories of human endurance and survival over time, but in this case my chances were nil.

Barring, of course, another miracle. And to fulfill his own purposes, the Lord would do just that. You see, he still had work for me to do. He still had great lessons for you and me to learn, and I was the man he would use to record this account under his divine inspiration.

This brings us to a famous verse and an event that is probably most often thought of when my name comes up: **"But the LORD provided a great fish to swallow Jonah, and Jonah was inside the fish three days and three nights" (1:17).**

Will there ever be an end to the amazing stories of how our great God provides? For Adam and Eve, the first promise of a Savior. For Noah and his family, instructions to build an ark. For God's Old Testament people, signs: a virgin would conceive and have a child, a child would be born in a feeding trough in Bethlehem, and many others. Escape from the oppression of slavery straight through the sea; food for thousands from a couple of loaves of barley and five small fish; and as many examples as there are people who trust his great promises, multiplied many times over by the number of stories that every child of God could tell.

And so in yet another amazing way the Lord provided, and he saved my life. I was near death when the Lord provided the fish. The Lord not only saved me, he then preserved me inside the great creature for three days and three nights. Appointing a great fish to carry out his great purpose might at first tempt us to think God was operating with an intriguing sense of humor. But in reality he had a marvelous purpose in mind.

Shortly I'll share with you my prayer from inside the belly of the fish. That will make it clear that I was near death when the Lord provided the fish. The Lord not only saved me, he then preserved me inside the fish for three days and three nights.

Do you remember how I pointed out some remarkable comparisons between me and my situation and Jesus? My being singled out to die in order to save the sailors will remind you of Jesus as will the immediate peace and calm that my being sacrificed brought. We can't say necessarily that in those details I was a sign, or type, of the coming Jesus, but we can say this about my three days in the belly of the fish. Jesus said that those three days were a sign of the three days he would lay in the grave after his death before the grave gave him back up: *"For as Jonah was three days in the belly of a huge fish, so the Son of Man will be three days and three nights in the heart of the earth" (Matthew 12:41).*

Just as I would be delivered from death after three days in the depths of the fish, so Jesus would be raised from death after three days of being buried in the earth. Jesus said that I was a sign of his glorious Resurrection that was soon to come.

## Inside the fish

This brings us to the second of the four chapters in the book of Jonah. What the Spirit led me to record is my cry from the depths, my emotional but faith-based prayer from inside the belly of this enormous fish. That my prayer is recorded here will tip you off at this point that I would make it out alive. **"From inside the fish Jonah prayed to the LORD his God" (2:1).**

Let me separate my prayer into three parts and present it to you one part at a time.

> He said, "In my distress I called to the LORD
> and he answered me.
> From the depths of the grave I called for help
> and you listened to my cry.
> You hurled me into the deep,
> into the very heart of the seas
> and the currents swirled about me;
> all your waves and breakers
> swept over me.
> I said, 'I have been banished
> from your sight.
> Yet I will look again
> toward your holy temple"
> (2:2-4).

In writing these words, I am recalling and recording what I was praying inside the fish. And inside the fish I was recalling my thoughts as I was swirling around in the deep. The water was about to be my grave. Although I had accepted my fate while still aboard the ship, I naturally still prayed for help as I sunk to the depths of the sea.

In the opening verse of my prayer, I praise God for listening to my pleadings at the bottom of the sea and answering my call for help. How had God done that? Well, I had expected to die as a consequence of my sin, though I trusted that my soul would be saved. But I was alive inside that fish, and that's evidence that God had saved both body and soul.

Some critics of the Bible in your time assume I was praising God for delivering me from the fish, and therefore assume that another later author penned these words and inserted them here. But that doesn't make sense. No, it is important to see that from inside the fish, I am praising God for having sent the fish to swallow me and bring me up from the depths of the sea.

It might not be the kind of Mediterranean cruise you would want to book, but no matter! God had saved me from death, and he had also preserved my soul during the storm by bringing me to repentance. How amazing that I experienced such profound joy while inside the belly of that creature of the deep!

*The original Biblical words for 'great fish' spoken of here and by Jesus in Mt. 12:40 are general enough to include any large sea creature. Here a whale shark pictured alongside a scuba diver highlights their relative size.*

## Out of the depths I cry

But before the joy, believe me, there was distress. My cry went out "from the depths of the grave." The Hebrew word for "grave" is "sheol" which sometimes also means "hell." As I sank to the bottom of the sea, distress came from the depths of my soul.

Perhaps you have prayed similar words or thoughts. Perhaps you too have felt such agony. It might have been grieving over a sin, and what that sin caused you to lose. Or it may have been heartache brought about by the kinds of events that rock people's lives—a tragic death, the prognosis of a terminal illness, the pain of a divorce, the loss of a job, a career, a home, or something else entirely. Yet, there was deliverance. And in time you could acknowledge that God was there and that he had heard your prayers.

In my prayer I continue describing my descent to the deep and my thoughts at the time. The currents were swirling around me. Notice how I accept responsibility for my actions, saying, *"You hurled me into the deep."* I knew it was God's will that the sailors throw me overboard. Even as I was near drowning, thoughts of deliverance came to my mind. They came in the form of words I had learned and prayed often. The wording of my thoughts was very similar to the Psalms of David, my opening words very similar to Psalm 30:2, 3. As the currents swirled around me, I thought, *"I have been banished from your sight. Yet I will look again toward your holy temple."*

My prayer continues:

> **"The engulfing waters threatened me,**
> **the deep surrounded me;**
> **seaweed was wrapped around my head.**
> **To the roots of the mountains I sank down,**
> **the earth beneath barred me in forever" (2:5-6a).**

It was on the ship that I hit rock bottom. Here in the water I did so physically. That's where you'll find seaweed, growing up from the bottom, and I was soon entangled. I had sunk down to the very "roots of the mountains." Recall that on the sea floor there are deep canyons as well as mountains, and I had landed at the bottom of a deep hole. There was no escape.

> **"But you brought my life up from the pit,**
> **O LORD my God.**
> **When my life was ebbing away**
> **I remembered you, LORD,**
> **and my prayer rose to you,**
> **to your holy temple (2:6b-7)."**

My life was "ebbing away," but my faith was so deeply rooted that with my faintest presence of mind I reached out for all that was left: "I remembered you, Lord." See, that's exactly what saving faith is. It does nothing—it can do nothing. It is nothing more than a pleading look. It is a hand into which the most invaluable gift imaginable is placed. Faith was simply my mind and heart remembering my gracious Lord.

Do you remember "the LORD," that is, the meaning of his name? It's worth bringing back to mind again. Remember, it comes from Exodus 34: *"The LORD, the LORD, the gracious and compassionate God, slow to anger, abounding in love and faithfulness, and forgiving wickedness, rebellion, and sin."* I use his name three times in my prayer.

Praying in faith in the living God draws one close to him. From deep inside that belly I drew strength from God as my bond with him became like a reinforced steel cable. A bolt of lightning would have paled in comparison to the power surge happening here. It was as though I was plugged into a million volts of electricity. Buoyed by no less than the power of the Spirit on high, my prayer gathers steam and roars to climactic triumph!

**"Those who cling to worthless idols**
**forfeit the grace that could be theirs.**
**But I, with a song of thanksgiving,**
**will sacrifice to you.**
**What I have vowed I will make good.**
**Salvation comes from the LORD!" (2:8-9).**

From inside the fish, I conclude my prayer. Again, it was not a petition for deliverance from the fish. It was a song of gratitude and praise, as well as a vow to serve God again, for I implicitly believed that I would see the light of day again. You see, the Lord and I were back on the same page!

# - 6 -

# Deliverance

**"A**nd the LORD commanded the fish, and it vomited Jonah onto dry land"** (2:10). Do you see how abundantly clear it is that this is the Lord's story? He called his prophet to a mission, directed the winds and waves, guided the casting of the lots, commissioned a fish for a special purpose, and the ordered the fish to give up its prey!

Does not the Lord always stand ready to deliver his people? He brought down the walls of Jericho; he parted the waters of the Red Sea; he gave victory to Gideon's three hundred men who faced an enemy of a hundred twenty thousand. In the midst of my flailing anxiety God gave me the calm confidence that he would hear my prayer for deliverance, and he did. He delivered me from the jaws of that massive amphibian.

But he delivered me from far more than that, didn't he? In fact if you reflect on my prayer, you'll remember that he had moved me to pray, *"I have been banished from your sight; yet I will look again toward your holy temple."* Because of my rebellion, I deserved banishment from God's sight. That's what hell is—total separation from God. Yet in that very moment

I retained the absolute certainty that he would spare me, that he would freely and fully forgive, that I would live to worship him again.

That's the full story of God's deliverance, isn't it? God has delivered us from evil, the very deliverance for which Jesus taught his disciples to pray. What I mean to say is that the Lord delivers us from our spiritual enemies. He delivers us from the guilt of our sin. He delivers us from death, the consequence of our sin. He delivers us from the power of the evil one, the devil, and his legions, who are hell bent on our destruction.

But such deliverance came at a cost. That's the very message you and I have been called to share with the world. The cost was the blood of God's only Son. Jesus delivered us by enduring death and hell in our place. All of Old Testament Scripture points ahead to the cross of Christ, and all of New Testament Scripture points back to it.

God promised deliverance the moment sin entered the world. He said to Satan in his serpent form, *"I will put enmity between you and the woman, between your seed and hers; he will crush your head, and you will bruise his heel"* (Genesis 3:15).

God's Son would become fully human so that God's moral law would apply to him, and so that he could die. Yet Jesus would be fully God so that his death could count as a substitute for our own, and so that he could defeat death and rise again. God's plan would be to take our sin on himself and to give us his holiness which we receive in exchange through faith in what he would do for us in Jesus, and in your case, through faith in what he has done for you in Jesus.

And so *"God made (Jesus) who knew no sin to become sin for us, so that in him we might become the righteousness of God"* (2 Corinthians 5:21). He "became sin," became like us sinners, taking our place, while we, on the other hand, through faith, receive credit for his holiness. Our sins are covered before God because over them we wear the robe of his righteousness. We are credited with his righteousness. *"This righteousness from God comes through faith in Jesus Christ to all who believe" (Romans 3:22).*

The story of our deliverance has been aptly called "The Greatest Story Ever Told." Christmas is all about our deliverance, celebrating the birth of the Savior of the world. Good Friday is all about our deliverance, how Jesus gave up his life to endure death and hell—separation from his Father—on the cross, in our place. Easter Sunday is about our deliverance, celebrating Jesus' resurrection, which proves that God accepted Jesus' payment and that he will raise our bodies from the grave on the last day.

And that brings us full circle, where God reinstates me for mission and ministry again here at the end of the second chapter and the precise midway point of this inspired Old Testament book.

# - 7 -

# Mission

"Then the word of the LORD came to Jonah a second time: 'Go to the great city of Nineveh and proclaim to it the message I give you'" (3:1,2).

Isn't it fascinating that I didn't get fired? How did I not get a pink slip after my performance? Why didn't I hear those words so often spoken: "I'm going to have to let you go." I mean when God calls, is showing up for work optional?

God is gracious. That's our answer, isn't it? And grace, of course, is love that is not deserved. Rather than finding someone else, God recommissioned me as his ambassador to Assyria. In fact the Lord never even brought up the subject of my disobedience. The Lord truly does forgive and forget. We'll have to see as the account unfolds whether my experience would make me an even better instrument for this mission than before.

## My message to Nineveh

God had not yet specifically mentioned the message I was to proclaim. It would be shared with me on the way.

**"Jonah obeyed the word of the LORD and went to Nineveh. Now Nineveh was a very large city; it took three days to go all through it. Jonah started into the city, going a day's journey and he proclaimed: 'Forty more days and Nineveh will be destroyed'" (3:3,4).**

My repentance was genuine. At this point, I wouldn't be characterized as "all talk, no action." I wasn't blowing smoke. I listened to the Lord and followed him. I embarked on my journey to the capital city of Assyria, a journey of some six hundred miles, the approximate distance from Chicago to Atlanta, which, of course, I traveled on foot.

Clearly, the message I was to proclaim was an urgent one. It was a most dire warning. God would destroy the city of Nineveh, but that destruction would only follow a period of forty days. Those eight words, *"Forty more days and Nineveh will be destroyed,"* embodied God's message throughout salvation history, that is, for all time. They are a proclamation of those two core biblical truths, law and gospel.

Law defines right and wrong; it is what human beings are morally accountable to do; and it states the punishment for disobedience. The message of law in my proclamation to the city is summarized by the words, *"Nineveh will be destroyed."* What that said was that the inhabitants were all guilty of sin before God. In God's first call to me he had said, *"Go to the great city of Nineveh and preach against it, because its wickedness has come up before me."* What this brief statement also said was that the punishment of death and eternal hell would soon be visited upon them as a result of their sin.

Gospel on the other hand is the opposite. It is not what people do for God, but rather what God has done for the world in Jesus. God dearly loved every one of the inhabitants of this city, and he wanted to save them from that destruction. His promise to send his Son as the Savior of the world was as sure and certain as if it had already taken place. The proclamation of law and gospel together is a proclamation of the

Bible's message; above all else, this is God's message to every human being of all time.

And of these two teachings, it is the gospel that is to have the upper hand. The law points out sin and the need for a Savior; the gospel proclaims that the Savior has come. The gospel message for the people of my time was that the Savior was on his way. It was a message that he would save us from sin, death, and the power of the devil. It was the wondrous news that he would win for us forgiveness for our sins and eternal life in heaven, blessings that we would receive solely through faith in the merits of Jesus on our behalf.

The gospel message to Nineveh is summarized in the words, *"Forty more days…"* Nineveh deserved immediate destruction, as has every soul since Adam and Eve. Every sunrise and sunset marks another day in God's time of grace, a time whereby God refrains from punishing and grants his people opportunity to receive him as their Lord and King.

Those eight words then would be only a summary and theme of my message. My message would have included proclaiming who the true God was, and that I was relaying God's message at his command. It would have included a proclamation of right and wrong and how the people of Nineveh were violating the natural law of God written in their hearts. I would then have proclaimed God's specific promise to send his Son to save them from their sins. And then it would have held out to them his invitation to believe it.

And so I set out on my three day preaching circuit, proclaiming God's message to the people of this mighty metropolis. Up and down the main streets of the city I went, wherever people tended to gather.

My message was brief and to the point. It put God in the foreground. As much the center of attention that I became, my faithful handling of God's Word allowed me to step into the background so that the thoughts of my hearers would not be on the messenger or the way in which it was delivered but on the substance of the message itself. That's what made it an effective message.

## The power of God's word

And what a dramatic effect it had! I had only started going into the city. I had only walked the streets with my message for one day. But listen to its impact: **"The Ninevites believed God. They declared a fast, and all of them from the greatest to the least, put on sackcloth. When the news reached the king of Nineveh, he rose from his throne, took off his royal robes, covered himself with sackcloth and sat down in the dust"** (3:5,6).

By now you are getting accustomed to hearing about the great miracles of the Lord in this episode of my life. This is another mighty miracle. But doesn't this sound like one of the greatest miracles of all time? The conversion of a single soul is a greater thing than God's creation of all the planets and all the stars and galaxies beyond our world—for they were made purely for our benefit. But the conversion of a half million people in one day? It is astounding!

An altar call in one of your churches today may result in many stepping forward, but for most it will likely be a God-pleasing act of dedication, a Spirit-moved commitment by people who have already come to know and believe in Jesus as their Savior. But here was a city full of people who had probably heard very little or nothing of the true God. How could so many come to know and believe in one day?

In Luke 11:30 Jesus said that I was a sign to the Ninevites. Perhaps word of my deliverance from the fish reached them before I did. At any rate, the message I proclaimed grabbed their attention, and the news spread instantly. People flocked to hear me. And while crowds can be fickle, it is also true that people of faith, even people of newborn faith, encourage one another. A coal put on fire will start to glow, but coals heaped on top of one another heat each other up and glow far more brightly.

Together the people of Nineveh declared a fast and put on sackcloth. Fasting was an act of self-denial; sackcloth was a scratchy, uncomfortable garment of camel's hair. These were symbolic acts that expressed the confession of their hearts and undoubtedly their lips. And though this is a personal matter of the heart, as a people they were smitten and stricken by the proclamation of God's law. And they were united in their repentance and faith in his forgiveness.

They mutually encouraged one another, and a great deal of that encouragement came from a leader. When news of my arrival and message reached the king of the most powerful nation on earth, he joined the people in expressing his sorrow over his sin and his trust in the true God who had just been revealed to him. He took off his royal robes, put on sackcloth of his own, stepped down from his throne, and sat down among his subjects on the dust of the ground. But not before he gathered his people together before God and gave voice to the people's commitment to a new way of life in keeping with the change that had been worked in their hearts.

> **"Then he issued a proclamation in Nineveh:**
> **'By the decree of the king and his nobles:**
> **Do not let any man or beast, herd or flock, taste**
> **anything; do not let them eat or drink. But let man**
> **and beast be covered with sackcloth. Let everyone**
> **call urgently on God. Let them give up their evil**
> **ways and their violence. Who knows? God may yet**
> **relent and with compassion turn from his fierce**
> **anger so that we will not perish'" (3:7-9).**

## Fruits of repentance

In his city wide observance, sackcloth was even to be put on the animals. Why put it on them? In that culture, the animals owned were viewed as an extension of the people themselves.

Even as deliverance followed my own repentance and faith, so deliverance happens again as God's mission to Nineveh carried out by his ambassador bore fruit in the lives of these Assyrian people. **"But when God saw what they did and how they turned from their evil ways, he had compassion and did not bring upon them the destruction he had threatened" (3:10).**

The Lord had compassion. How remarkable is that! Remember that his moral standards are high, and his justice is perfect. His standard is moral perfection, or he wouldn't be holy; he wouldn't be God. But his love is perfect, too. That means his love is a blazing fire, white hot in intensity. Only such a love would stand ready to place his only Son directly in the path of the consequence of sin. God would do that for Nineveh, so great was his compassion. Nineveh listened to that promise and as one people, they believed it. And into their open hands of Spirit worked faith was placed the greatest gift possible—forgiveness.

Oh, how I love such a Lord! And there's something else that boggles my mind. Think of what God accomplished through me, such a reluctant missionary! But isn't this exactly what God does, accomplishing great things through very imperfect people? And if at times our personal failures lead us to think God will not entrust us with a whole lot, shouldn't we think again?

God can, God wants to, and God will accomplish great things through us. That we merely go about our lives as forgiven children of God despite our past record of failures gives testimony of God's great mercy. People will relate to that, and our confidence in our own forgiveness will radiate soothing comfort. Our joy in the face of adversity will attract people who sense something missing in their lives and who feel a longing that grows every day.

Students of history among you might know that the Assyrian empire lasted for about 150 years, when Nineveh was destroyed in 612 B.C. by the Babylonian Empire. If you are a student of Bible history, you will know that corruption had set in again and that Nineveh fell by God's hand. We don't know to what degree faith in the true God was passed down to successive generations after that great conversion. Sometimes the faith of a nation's citizens wanes.

Yet the gospel endures. God promises, *"My word... will not return to me empty, but will accomplish what I desire and achieve the purpose for which I sent it" (Isaiah 55:11)*. Even when a nation loses its godliness, the gospel is still passed on in places and in lives in the land. And at the same time the Spirit of God moves on, the gospel moving like a rain cloud to a new place, watering seeds previously sown, and nurturing, growing, pruning and flourishing there.

Nevertheless in Nineveh a great number of souls were saved. What rejoicing among the angels! Jesus said, *"There is more rejoicing in heaven over one sinner who repents than over ninety-nine righteous persons who need no repentance" (Luke 15:7)*. Imagine the noise level in heaven when a half million souls were saved on this single day! And the celebration of the angels would have continued to resound as the passionate faith of the Ninevite people undoubtedly spread to many new places and people throughout the land, and as time went on, to their progeny as well.

And what a great day in my life too! Try to imagine the kind of emotion I might have felt as God used my humble obedience to bring about such an astounding result! People like to see the fruits of their labors; it tends to give them a feeling of fulfillment. As a prophet, I didn't always see the tangible results of my work, even though I felt great personal fulfillment in knowing that the Spirit works invisibly in people's hearts. Believe me, I found my work profoundly rewarding, privileged as I knew I was to serve as the Lord's ambassador, to proclaim a Word that I knew would give life to dying souls.

But a half million souls in one day! Here the dramatic evidence of the gospel's power was displayed in electrifying fashion! How truly rewarding would it be for anyone to be used to bring hundreds of thousands of souls into his kingdom. Saved from the belly of a fish for such a wonderful, wonderful role! How could this not have been the greatest day in my life?

Get prepared for another surprise.

# - 8 -

# Relapse

"**B**ut Jonah was greatly displeased and became angry. He prayed to the LORD, 'O LORD, is this not what I said when I was still at home? That is why I was so quick to flee to Tarshish. I knew that you are a gracious and compassionate God, slow to anger and abounding in love, a God who relents from sending calamity. Now, O LORD, take away my life, for it is better for me to die than to live" (4:1-3).

So begins the final chapter of the book of Jonah. Earlier we explored my initial mindset. Had my secret desire only been the demise of Assyria's power, I don't know that anyone would object. But when God wanted to spare their lives and win their souls, I became so afraid of them that I actually opposed God's will to save them. You know I'd been afraid of God as well, because I waited till now to tell God why I didn't want to go!

Though I had since repented, traces of my fear and frustration still remained. My weaknesses had been allowed to fester for some time, and vestiges of my warped thinking were still latent in my heart and soul.

Those residual fears were more than mood changers, they infiltrated my attitude and left me "greatly displeased" and angry.

Anger is often a manifestation of our fears. First we run from God because we're afraid of something that he allows in our lives or wants from us. Then, we gradually start to replace him by putting ourselves on the throne of our own hearts and lives. That makes it easier to be angry when things don't go the way they should.

But when sinful thoughts are left unchecked to any degree, Christians risk falling into the same sins over and over again. That's why regular contrition and repentance is so critical. Contrition is being sorry, and repentance is embracing God's forgiveness in Jesus and committing to change. Satan is a vicious predator, sniffing out our weak spots, eager to ensnare us. He *"prowls around like a roaring lion, seeking whom he may devour" (I Peter 5:8).*

What could I have done to prevent this situation? I had gotten in the way of God's great plans, and then I couldn't seem to get happy when God moved powerfully among souls. I finally verbalized my feelings, but my conversation was one sided. My thinking was, "This is not going to make me very popular at home. I'd rather die than witness such a thing." I was ready to die even before I gave God a chance to speak to the issue. I cried out, *"Take away my life, for it is better for me to die than to live."*

I should have resolved my feeling long before this. Certainly I had every right to be angry with the brutality and unfair aggression of the Assyrians. But the bigger picture was that God loves all people and that Israel's role was still to live godly lives and showcase the Messiah for all the other nations. I and my people needed to look at ourselves first. We needed to repent and turn back to God before pointing our collective finger at Assyria. Had I kept this perspective, I would have obeyed God and prayed that both nations would turn to the LORD and live.

But instead, just at the climactic moment of truth when my secret desire was about to go permanently unfulfilled, I relapsed. When we relapse, pent up feelings and emotions are often released. In a distorted frame of mind, we give in to what we desire, what we think must be, what we think we must have. But the truth catches up with us quickly, and whatever we've turned to for escape does not fulfill. The floodgates open and disappointment rushes in, sometimes so deep that it becomes a feeling of despair.

## A most patient God

So what was God's response to this? Did he wince and roll his eyes? Well, if God could be patient with half a million Assyrians, could he still have patience now? He'd been patient with me before. Perhaps my chances weren't all that bad, wouldn't you say?

**"But the LORD replied, 'Have you any right to be angry?"** **(4:4).** There's no punishment here, no frustrated "if you say so." He merely asked a probing question that got to the root of the issue. In the word "discipline" we hear the related word "disciple." I was still a disciple, though sometimes confused and misguided. Literally the word "disciple" means "follower" or "learner." At the heart of the word "discipline" is the concept of teaching. Teaching and correcting are discipline's loving purpose, and this was the Lord's sole purpose in dealing with me.

He gave me time to reflect on that question. I knew the answer, but that doesn't mean I felt better. This isn't the first time you saw me angry at God and his ideas and plans, but notice that at this point I never professed a right to be angry. I just admitted that I was.

If you can identify with me at all, maybe you can relate to what I did next. The logical thing would have been to move on, right, perhaps to go home. Clearly God had made his decision. He had backed off of his threat and poured out forgiving grace for Jesus' sake. The decision was blessedly final.

But I didn't go home. I guess you could say I was just too mixed up. **"Jonah went out and sat down at a place east of the city. There he made himself a shelter, sat in its shade and waited to see what would happen to the city" (4:5).**

I know, I know. It was time to let it go. But relapse is a powerful thing. And that first step back is always the hardest. I needed to admit that I was wrong and I just had to step down off the throne that belongs to God.

I think the most beautiful thing in the world is how God reaches out to those he loves. God was not about to lose me. Like the patient teacher that he is, he came alongside me again. Sometimes what is needed is an object lesson. And that's what the Teacher constructed for the benefit of his beloved child.

**"Then the LORD made a vine and made it grow up over Jonah to give shade for his head to ease his discomfort, and Jonah was very happy about the vine" (4:6).** The first object God used was a vine, a kind of fast-growing plant with large enough leaves to give me ample shade from the hot sun. This was yet another miracle, a further demonstration of the almighty power God chooses to use to carry out his will. The plant grew to maturity in less than twenty-four hours.

Then the Teacher used another life form for his lesson, followed by the sun and the wind. Everything was at his disposal, for his purpose. **"But at dawn the next day God provided a worm, which chewed the vine so that it withered. When the sun rose, God provided a scorching east wind, and the sun blazed on Jonah's head so that he grew faint. He wanted to die, and said, "It would be better for me to die than to live" (4:7,8).**

Discipline usually isn't a lot of fun, is it? The writer to the Hebrews says, *"No discipline seems pleasant at the time, but painful. Later on, however, it produces a harvest of righteousness and peace for those who have been trained by it" (2:11)*. The step back into recovery is often not without some very unpleasant symptoms of withdrawal.

The demonstration portion of the lesson was now complete. The point of the lesson was to come. God returned to his original question, but now masterfully applied it to the vine. **"Do you have any reason to be angry about the vine?" (4:9a).**

The sun shines, the wind blows, we find shelter from the elements, but then we're subjected to the elements again. Such things are the stuff of life. But life became unpleasant and my anger flared up again. There's a pattern unfolding in my behavior, an inner attitude being revealed, and God helped me to face it head on.

## Still with me at rock bottom

And now I pour out all my feelings again. I answered the question I was asked. **"I do," he said, "I am angry enough to die" (4:9b).** My anger had been turned inward, creating feelings of despair. My feelings ran deep, and they had to come out. Up to this point I hadn't maintained that my anger was justified. Now I do. But my anger had been directed at a vine, and at some emotional level I think I was aware of its futility.

I was so deeply affected by the death of this plant, so totally frustrated that I had lost my comfortable spot in the shade, that at the moment I stated my right to be angry I also gave voice to my true emotion of despair. I honestly felt a desire to die, my despair had so leveled me.

Perhaps it wouldn't have been long before my anger at the plant would have likely found resolution. Perhaps I would have worked it through. But don't forget that the death of the vine was a structural component of a much greater lesson plan.

My answer to God's question is the final thing that you will hear me say.

"But what about a happy ending?" someone may wonder. "How can a book so wonderfully moving end with you speaking words like these? How can you be an inspiration to us when after all that God did for you, we still hear a stubborn, insolent statement like this—that you're "angry enough to die"—and it turns out to be the last thing you say?"

Perhaps you're sensing a good answer to those questions. You nailed it if you're thinking something like, "Well, this isn't really Jonah's story, after all." And of course, this isn't the end of the account either. The object lesson isn't yet complete. We still have two more verses to go.

And you know what? Isn't it more likely to be a happy ending when one lets God have the last word?

*An ancient depiction of the book of Jonah's sequence of events.*

# - 9 -

# Surrender

And that's exactly what I did. Yes, it's quite true that prophets are expected to talk, and that you too are compelled to speak to God in prayer and to people in your lives with words of love. Fair enough. But there's something more important still. Jesus said that to Martha, as her sister Mary sat at his feet, spellbound, hanging on his every Word: *"Only one thing is needed,"* Jesus said, *"and Mary has chosen what is better" (Luke 10:42).* In reality, what do you see in the book of Jonah's final scene? You see me listening to the Lord as he drives the point of his awesome lesson home.

**"But the LORD said, 'You have been concerned about this vine, though you did not tend it or make it grow. It sprang up overnight and died overnight. But Nineveh has more than a hundred and twenty thousand people who cannot tell their right hand from their left, and many cattle as well.**

**"Should I not be concerned about that great city?" (4:10).**

Indeed! It's understandable that a gardener who weeds and waters and prunes might be a little upset if his or her roses and tulips meet with a sudden end by hail or downpour or the accidental misstep of a child. There's a bit of an investment there, though the disappointment will rather quickly pass. But what was it that I held so dear to my heart? It was the fleeting shade of a plant that gave me some momentary comfort.

Now God cares for plants too, and animal life as well. He cares for the lilies of the field and cows and dogs and chipmunks and reindeer. Of sparrows Jesus said, *"Not one of them will fall to the ground apart from the will of your Father" (Matthew 10:29).*

But the point, of course, is this: if God did not discount my feeling, if he was OK with my intense grief over the death of a plant, then could not I grant God a feeling appropriately intense for the souls and lives of over a hundred twenty thousand children in a city of half a million people?

The book of Jonah ends perfectly, with God masterfully bringing home the great Truth in his lesson on his prophet's behalf. It is of course his Great Lesson for every man, woman and child.

He loves the gazelle that bounds through the trees unseen by anyone but him. How very intense indeed must his love be for you and me! How great is his grace and mercy and loving compassion for every person everywhere and of every time! With a blazing passion he loves the very people who mock, scorn, and jeer at him the most, even those who hate and hurt and commit the greatest of atrocities against his dear children.

Indeed, he does hold court as the Most Supreme Justice, but he has declared the world not guilty for Jesus' sake. He poured out his righteous fury for the worst of sins on his own Son, so that every sin of every man, woman and child might be stamped, "Paid in Full." He did that so that he might welcome and embrace every single man, woman and child who ever took a breath of life. This Great Christmas Gift, this Great "I love you," is set before every person, so that they may believe what he says and live with him forever!

As for me, what better ending for you to see of me in this episode than to see me attentively listen and learn. Sometimes we call it "surrender."

And then let me ask you to envision one more thing in the life of your brother in the faith. Picture me listening to the Lord again, as the Spirit of God breathed into me the words of this account that I wrote. Though it wouldn't paint the most flattering picture of me, I responded to this divine calling and recorded this Word of God for your benefit and blessing. And as I wrote, I knew it was to that very end that God would use my words.

You see, while on that side of heaven, and now on this side, I've been looking forward to meeting you!

# Conclusion:
# In His Hands

I was somewhere between six and eight years old, it's hard to pinpoint. The school I attended in Appleton, Wisconsin, was right across the street from where I lived, so I walked home from school on my own. Nevertheless, it was no short stroll for a little kid, especially when required to use sidewalks and crosswalks.

I have a pretty vivid memory of an incident that scared the dickens out of me. I was walking down the sidewalk halfway home when I heard someone behind me yell, "Hey!" in a voice that was menacing, or at least that's the way I perceived it. I turned around to see a single student walking about twenty feet behind, someone I didn't know. He was clearly younger and definitely smaller than me, yet he must have been convinced that he could and should beat me up. I'm sure of it because he said something to that effect, though I can't recall the words. I do remember that somehow he looked and sounded tough, a word that I don't think had ever been used to describe me.

I do remember the terror. I remember a lifelong pattern of avoiding conflict emerging already then. I definitely remember wanting to run and hide. I remember breaking into a sprint and eventually getting knocked down. And I remember looking up at him not in anger but in stark fear. Apparently that was enough for him, because he walked away. I ran home bawling and poured out my story, probably sounding like a kid scared of his shadow.

It's fear of course that makes us want to flee. Fear paralyzes us. Fear comes from the unknown. Asking for a date, asking for a raise, confronting someone who is doing wrong. Fear makes us flee situations, problems, conflicts, life.

For Jonah this included immediate physical flight. He fled straight to the nearest port to get on the nearest ship to Anywhere. The way he saw it, once aboard a boat, he bore no more responsibility. That would soothe his guilt feelings. Even if he changed his mind, the itinerary of a voyage is generally quite established by departure time. One cannot get a ship's captain to simply spin the vessel around for a temporary detour.

A good number of decades after that episode with the little bully, I still knew how to escape. In the moments I felt I couldn't cope, I made decisions to seek relief. I knew exactly how to get it in the quickest way. I knew what to reach for in order to find instant relief from the stress, the hurt feelings, the beleaguered pride, the pain of shaken self image, the horror of tragedy, the burdens of responsibility. I became the artful dodger, fairly expert at running from whatever it was I thought I needed to flee.

Regardless of where our drugs of choice fit along the vast panorama of wayward thoughts, activities, or manufactured experiences we may turn to for help, our own personal escape to them is a flight from God that interrupts our own inclination to live responsibly. When we are being responsible, our issues are always resolved. We find fulfillment and we feel good about our achievements, our service, our contributions to society. We feel good about ourselves.

But there have been times along the way when we abandoned this because of attendant difficulties and burdens, whatever they might have been. We became too tired, exhausted, or burnt out to keep up. Yet at the root of these feelings is fear.

It may be subconscious but ultimately we were afraid to face our problems head on, afraid to trust God's promises fully. We were afraid to take him at his word when he promised, *"We know that in all things God works for the good of those who love him, who are called according to his purpose" (Romans 8:28)*. We were afraid to live out our faith on any given day with the kind of reckless abandon that comes from placing ourselves fully in his care, *"to take captive every thought to make it obedient to Christ" (2 Corinthians 10:5)*. This is what Jonah was afraid to do.

For some of us, the cycle went something like this. We found easier ways to feel good. In fact, we discovered instant gratification. But the truth we had trouble seeing is how utterly empty these false gods are. There was no lasting fulfillment, no resolution of issues, and in fact only the piling up of unmet responsibilities.

And then, as though we had fallen too far behind, we were on a ship headed the wrong way. We turned to God for forgiveness, and it was ours. But we weren't used to the right thought patterns that would get us on a better course to fulfill our responsibilities once more and so we often circled back into a cycle of yielding to pain, reaching for our escape, feeling our despair and just giving up and giving in until the fruitlessness of it all brought us to reality, and we turned to God again.

Yes, fear sometimes leads us to flee from God and his will for us. It's human nature to want to escape sometimes. But if you've ever felt that you've been running from God or avoiding his will for you, I pray the book of Jonah has given you a measure of encouragement and comfort.

A counselor once asked me, "What are you running from?" Among other things, that question eventually made me think of Jonah, which in turn became the inspiration for this book. What the book of Jonah shows me most clearly is what it is that can break through fear. It is love that breaks through fear and inspires courage. And there's an ancient proverb that says fear and courage are brothers. Courage, someone else once said, is nothing more than fear saying its prayers.

Love conquers fear. Love broke through and saved Jonah from his fear. God's love touches our hearts, souls, and minds in a way that can conquer all fears forever. The love of God for us and in us works through us. It inspires us to love others. We will still work to get our human needs met, needs like attention, validation, and acceptance, but love from others is out of our control. As we focus on loving those who are in our lives, we can let go of the urge to seek love; it will come as a gift.

The love of God in Jesus is transforming. It impacts, renews and completely remakes the very way we think of ourselves. The absolutely unconditional love of God gives us a brand new identity.

You see, there may be a time and a situation today where I find myself cowering. But that doesn't mean I have to think of myself as a coward. Because that's not how God sees me; that's not my identity. There will be another time when I fail, or when I can rightly say, "At the moment I am failing at this," but it makes no sense for me to think "I am a failure." You may have even committed a felony, but that's already in the past. You don't have to think of yourself as a felon. You don't even have to wear the label "ex-offender."

When God forgives our sin, he no longer identifies us by it, and we don't have to either. Everyone has many moral weaknesses, sins that they repeat often, but they don't need to define themselves by them. Neither do we then have to define ourselves as cheaters, liars, delinquents, adulterers, loudmouths, or even murderers.

You see, the best thing to do is reject the labels that God no longer uses for us in Jesus and retain the labels and noble descriptions that he uses for us in his Word.

In the second last chapter of Luke we have one of the accounts of Jesus' crucifixion, and under inspiration the gospel writer relates that two thieves were crucified on either side of him. At that time "thief" was the perfect word to use for both of them regardless of how many thefts they committed. At the time what indication was there that anything about them was changed?

But Luke relates how one of them did change, and was changed. After his partner in crime and others mocked Jesus, we hear this: *"But the other criminal rebuked him. 'Don't you fear God?' he said. 'We are punished justly, for we are getting what our deeds deserve. But this man has done nothing wrong.' Then he said, 'Jesus, remember me when you come into your kingdom.' Jesus answered him, 'Today you will be with me in Paradise'"* (Luke 23:40-43).

In the moment he turned in newborn faith to his LORD, he, too, was not so much a thief as he was a saint. For the word "saint" means "a person who is made holy." The only way one is made holy is to be declared holy through faith in Jesus. The "thief on the cross" was still a sinner like all of us, but like us, our brother in the faith was a child of God, a brother of Jesus, a citizen of heaven to be seated side by side with missionaries, apostles and Christian mothers at the Great Banquet Feast of the Lamb.

So how long is a thief a thief? If you or I shoplifted a baseball or a bag of M & M's when we were nine, are we still thieves? I would not think of you that way, nor would I even be inclined to think of you as a criminal if that were the nature of any of your sins—no matter what your offense was. I wouldn't be inclined to think of you as a bully, a cheapskate, an alcoholic, a traitor, a con man, an addict, or a dummy. I would think of you as a brother or sister in the faith.

The point is, labels are often far from helpful. The key is to apply a label to yourself if and when it is. It may be helpful to think of yourself as any one of those things we mentioned when you need to boldly face truth rather than to flee truth. In that case, it may well indeed be helpful for me to think of myself as a procrastinator, a slowpoke, a daydreamer, a high stakes risk taker, a selfish individual, or any label that may now or may have applied to any of the vices to which I may have been or may be addicted. It is most certainly helpful for me to apply to myself the label of sinner, because I am that and will continue to be that every day.

But the reason that is helpful and necessary is so that I might know and believe that I am a forgiven sinner. That is how the Lord thinks and speaks of me, and that then is how I think and speak of myself. And that is how you can think of yourself, too.

Like this: I am a child of God. I am a Christian. I am a disciple. I am a saint. I am a new creation. I am an ambassador who speaks in God's name. I am a steward of all that God gives me. I am a missionary, sent by him to share his saving love with my children, my family, those in my world, and those beyond in any way I can. I am even now a citizen of heaven.

God uses beautiful, thought-provoking pictures of who I am in his eyes. I am the light of the world and the salt of the earth. I am a living stone in the spiritual house that God builds, that is, his church. The Christian church is also called the body of Christ, and I am a member of that body. I am part of *"a chosen people, a royal priesthood, a holy nation, a people belonging to God"* (I Peter 2:9).

Every day I can remember not only what he calls me but all that he says about me. I am forgiven. I am born again. I am free from condemnation. I was bought with a price, the ransom demanded by sin, death, and Satan. I am renewed in the image of God. I stand justified before him, declared righteous and innocent of all wrong. I am grafted into Jesus, rooted in Christ, adopted into God's family. I am totally empowered, someone who can say as Paul did, *"I can do everything through him who gives me strength" (Philippians 4:13).*

It doesn't matter how we feel in the moment. What matters is how God sees us and who and what he says we are. There is no better antidote to the fear that sometimes makes us want to run away from it all.

Word came to me one day that my oldest son, who was twelve, was in a very serious car accident. Home with my other children, I needed to wait by the phone for further details. Like it was yesterday I remember my thoughts, my feelings, my intense fear as I waited. Very specifically I remember my mind immediately choosing a path, instantly coming to believe that I could never cope, never survive if the worst had happened. It was very understandable, very normal, but it was still raw fear, a refusal to face a possibility, one that my gracious God might permit.

Three families lost loved ones on that excruciating day, while my son alone escaped serious injury. By the grace of God I was permitted to see powerful examples of human survival and faith, amidst the hardest kind of trauma ever felt, within the two families that I was so privileged to know. For this I am forever indebted.

Five and a half years later, I again stood under the protective umbrella of God's amazing grace when I received word that my second son, also twelve, had suddenly died. It was then that I learned that I had been wrong.

It was then that God's love in Jesus was indelibly imprinted on my heart like never before. My youngest brother was the first to speak powerful and perfect words of profound comfort. My oldest nephew wrote "Fly Away: David's Song" while traveling on his band's farewell tour, which he sang for the funeral. Then the words of parents who had also lost children were an absolute oasis of triage for my heart, and the support of hundreds of others were like hands pulling me out of quicksand.

The darkest days, months, and years of my life followed, but one single fact anchored itself in my heart and soul, like a high-tech steel girded building withstanding a hurricane that slams our Eastern coastline or the ravaging power of a tsunami. It was the very same truth, resounding and reverberating through heart, mind, and soul, that had safely moored so many others who had suffered such intense loss, so often expressed in nearly the same words: "I cannot imagine how anyone could face this without faith in Jesus."

Yes, that intimate faith I shared with those parents, that foolproof knowledge that my Buddy Boy is forever alive, safe in the bosom of his Savior, has been a constant and powerful Beacon of light, of peace, and of hope. Light gradually overcame the darkness, and Love slowly evaporated the fear.

You and I bask in the perfect love of our Savior. We need never run, for we rest secure in his boundless grace. We need never hide, because we can stand boldly before God, who has hidden all our sins from his sight. We need never pursue elusive searches for happiness and fulfillment, for we are invited to seek, ask, and knock on heaven's door.

With the majestic Lord of the universe at our side, we can always face our problems. We can always face our pasts. We can always face ourselves.

In fact, we can face anything!

CPSIA information can be obtained at www.ICGtesting.com
Printed in the USA
267916BV00001B/130/P